We Are Here

Collected Poems

GREG HART

MILAGRO CORN COMPANY
Tucson, Arizona

Copyright © 2026 Greg Hart

All rights reserved under domestic and international copyright.

Outside of fair use (such as quotation within a book review), no part of this publication may be reproduced, stored in a retrieval system, used to educate AI, or transmitted in any form or by any means, electronic, mechanical, photocopying, recording, or otherwise, without the written permission of the publisher.
For permissions, please contact: Milagro Corn Company, ClaireScheuren@gmail.com

Published by Milagro Corn Company
Crane illustration by Ilyas Ahmed

Paperback ISBN 978-0-9796921-4-7
Hardback ISBN 978-0-9796921-5-4

Four poems in this edition were published previously in *Sixfold Summer 2023:* "Not the Longing," "At the Altar of Being," "False Coordinates," and "Leo of St. David."

For

VICKI

since the beginning

Contents

I found nothing.
Nothing, in fact, found me.
Everything is here.

—G.H.

Leo of St. David

Tonight, at dinner in a little Greek restaurant, my wife, Vicki, said, "Have you seen my husband lately?"

"Yes, I have. I am your husband."

She laughed a little and said, "I must be losing my mind."

And, of course, she is. Even though she can't always put our relationship in context, she still speaks to me as her most trusted friend, and that is maybe the most important thing right now.

At dinner tonight, she tried so hard with so much courage and humor to contextualize her life and our life together with our sons.

"Where do they live?" she asked. "Do they come to see us? Are they married? I know I have known them a long time, and I did my best, did a lot of things with them. I was with them. I know I love them."

"You were a wonderful mother. They were everything to you. You gave them everything, and they are happy and good men because of you."

"I am happy I can talk to you this way. It is important for me."

"Me, too."

"Please help me," she said, "if I do anything stupid."

"Like what?"

"If I hurt them in any way."
"I will."

Last weekend, we went to see the sandhill cranes at Whitewater Draw in southeastern Arizona with our friends, Jerome and Sue. They have been at our side, unfaltering in the face of this change, the loss and the harbinger of more loss it represents.

The sandhill crane migration is one of a dwindling number of mass animal migrations, and watching it is as awe-inspiring as it is a sad reminder of what we have lost and are losing. We went last year, too.

I wrote a poem about it with the refrain, "We are here…," which I think sounds like the cry of the cranes as they come down to land on the water. Here it is.

The Coming and Going of Cranes

Sandhill cranes, elegant
as the concubine's kimono,
forming at first like barely visible
wisps of smoke undulating
over the mountains
in the eastern
desert haze of midmorning
and then and coming and coming
in wave after

wave, hour after hour
to this desert wetland,
fed by water
flowed down
from the mountains
that had been
still, at rest in the
aquifer for 4,000,000 years,

cranes coming and coming
with their jubilant, insistent
cries, we are here, we are here,
we are here in the world,
come to this resting and feeding place,
just like the 10,000 generations
before came and came
and came.
We are here. We are here.

We have been married for fifty years. Not so long. It does not seem at all long.

There are moments now when she does not remember the names of our sons. We are sitting side by side on the edge of the wetland, looking up into the gyre of 1,000 sandhill cranes descending in striations from above, some moving clockwise, others counterclockwise, we are here, gliding down, their gilded underwings sliding through the cloudless blue, so elegant, so much more here that is true in this golden, trilling whirlwind than can be described and codified by deadenders, poets, philosophers, priests, and gurus.

We don't know where we've been, why we are, or where we are going. The cranes see us better than we see them, know what we've done, what we can do.

> It is all so ancient,
> so maddeningly real, this jubilant swirl, so familiar, but
> so very brief.
> Yet, we are here.
> We are here.

On the way back from the cranes this year, we stopped at a little roadside stand in St. David, Arizona, which was founded in the 1870s by Mormon settlers, or members of the Church of Latter-Day Saints, as they now prefer to be called. It is just a little bit down the road from the much-better-known town of Tombstone.

There are now about 1,600 people living there. It sits near the banks of the San Pedro River, one of the last living, perennial rivers in Arizona. But it is only a river by desert standards, which means it has water in it, albeit just enough at times to get your feet wet.

The largest building in St. David is the Stake House of the Latter-Day Saints, just off Highway 80. Farther down Highway 80 a bit, on the other side of the road, is the Catholic Holy Trinity Monastery.

We pulled up to the roadside stand beneath the winter-bare cottonwoods. The sun was getting lower, and it was soft on the pond behind the stand. We had the barest of breezes. The stand had one-pound bags of seasoned pistachios for sale—salted, unsalted, garlic, peppered, chipotle, and more, with free samples so you could make an informed choice.

Leo was the proprietor, a diffident but approachable man in a beaten-up straw hat, a hard-used T-shirt, and a pair of suspenders holding up his jeans. He would lift his hand a little as the cars passed, a small gesture but, I suspect, an effective one.

Leo had some pecans, too, and a sign advertised honey for sale, but I didn't see any honey on the table.

"Do you have honey?" I asked him.

"I do. Can't sell it on Sunday."

I didn't think I'd heard him correctly. "What? What do you mean?"

"Can't sell it on Sunday. Can't have it on the table."

"Why?"

"Man who produces the honey's wife died, and he married a younger woman, fifteen years younger, and she says we can't sell it on Sundays. We used to, but then the first wife died, and he does what the new wife wants. There's no law in the Bible that says you can't sell honey on Sunday."

"Oh," I said. "Well, do you have any around?"

"Yeah, over in the trailer."

We walked over to the trailer, where Leo reached in and took out a bottle of honey for me. I asked him if he would mind if we had a little picnic behind his stand, and he said go right ahead. Help yourself.

Later, when we were having our picnic on the soft tree duff, in the dappled shade, I could see Leo lifting his arm in a little diffident wave at the passing cars. I put some of the Sunday honey on a slice of apple and had the thought that this was the best honey I'd ever tasted.

I went back over to the stand to get a bag of pistachios, and Leo and I talked a little.

He didn't eat the pistachios, he said. "Don't have any teeth." And then I noticed that was a fact. He didn't smile at all. "My dad had the same problem. "Lost his teeth early. But he ate pistachios anyway."

"How'd he do that?" I asked.

"He gummed 'em to death, I guess," Leo said and almost smiled.

He was from Boston, had been in St. David for thirty-seven years. Would have never known that by looking at him, but what do we ever really know by looking at someone?

He didn't make or grow the pistachios, but got them from the monastery. He said he had had a rough year.

"What's going on?" I asked.

"Well, my wife died, then my son died two weeks later. Found him frozen behind the courthouse in Boston. And then my dog died, all within three weeks."

"That is hard," I said. "Very, very hard. Terrible. I am so sorry."

"Yes," he said. "Thank you. Life goes so fast." He looked at me directly. "In a nanosecond."

"Yes, I know."

And we did know that, between us there.

"Take care of yourself, Leo."

We shook hands.

"You, too."

"Take it easy, Leo," I called back as I walked to the car.

He lifted his hand a bit in recognition and turned back to waving at the cars going down the road in the settling light of the afternoon, beneath the winter-bare cottonwoods.

Not the Longing

It's just part of the deal.

Who doesn't want
a dog that will never die?
A home that will never fall?
A voice that will never crack?
Longing is the heart
of the long dream.
For a lost child,
a kinder mother.
A faithful brother.
A heart that
never skips a beat.
To be taller.
For unclenched teeth.
For health, enough to eat,
a final explanation.
You name it.
For the innocence.
the green fields,

the black earth,
where I lie,
a child humming with
the bees, hidden
in the fields of mustard,
in the life of the grasses,
in the life of the planet,
chewing the milky bases
of the blades
the sunny sweetness
running down my throat
that's become suddenly
a light sparked brook,
I become the sun,
the black earth, the grasses
and all of the around.
No discrimination, no separation.
I long
the lost nation.

For the high flying
circus life, bumbling,
clowning round the ring,
chasing my hat,
laughing, home with my kind,
my funny, flying friends?

For something upon which
nothing depends,
that will never unwind,
something that always stays.
Laughter is the finest satisfaction.
For a perfect lover
right from the dream,
right out of the sacred fire,
to fill the original
borderless space.
To whisper into
my perfect ear
with her perfect
electric mouth,
you are complete,
you are safe,
in this forever place,
you make me entire.
The ghost consummation.
What is it?
What is it
In this long dream?

Always alone,
finding a way
everywhere, everyway,
in the water,
across the cliff,
through the uncertain crowds,
there, in the dream,
to find a way,
to the culmination.

To be the life,
not the longing.
To be the life.

Beyond the Confines

Of course I want to be
as fantastic at those
pictures the Hubble
Telescope takes
of deep space!
Don't we all!
Like the Pillars of Creation,
for example!
Also known, in the astronomical
Nomenclature, as M-16,
NGC-6611,
the Eagle Nebulae!
The big pillar is
24 trillion miles high!
That's high!
No wonder it needs
so many big names!

Andromeda is the galaxy
closest to ours (we call it
the Milky Way! I wondered,
as a child, how you can see
what you are living in.
I still do).

Andromeda is 220,000
light years from edge to edge.
(Be mindful of man, that is
186,000 miles per second
or 220,000 years, and you'd
just be finishing up.)

Like my friend the bicyclist
said, my friend on the multiple
anti-psychotic medications,
my friend
with the gold streamers
glimmering from the ends
of the handlebars of his
hand-painted, gold-trimmed carbon-
wheeled, carbon-framed
$15,000 bicycle.

(Carbon, they say,
is the building block of life!)

He said
he doesn't like to read
about that sort of thing
anymore in the astronomy
magazines at the library.
"It's just too much, beyond me,"
he says. "What is the meaning
of largeness anyway?
Who needs it?

It's stupid. Why
does everything have
to be so large? I mean,
What's the point?"

He's just being honest.
Not many people stop
by his seat at Starbucks
to chat anymore—he's
bedraggled, the dye fading
from the ashen curls
like sepia gas rising
from a supernova,
his pastel riding outfits
dirty, sewn up, patched
with pictures of wolves, forms
of stars over his crotch.

You know, in the end,
I guess we should appreciate
the confines,
the boundaries that define us—
a lot of poets say they
want to go
beyond the confines,
talking a good game,
but who really
is prepared
to launch themselves out
alone,
out through the light years?

It's just not our place, now,
is it?
No, our place is
to point and marvel,
to huddle with the other animals,
to hold a hand and to have
a hand held, to sorrow,
to travel
the terribly short minute
to mercy.
That's our job,
right there.

Short Letter

You died with the ideals.
Funny how that works,
as if you were connected.

It rained two weeks ago.
First rain in seven months.
That was historic.
There's a lot of change,
a lot of dying going on.

I noticed it didn't sound
the same, the rain,
without you here
to hear it, too.
That was a surprise.
But if I had known,
I could have guessed that.

Now, I just say, the rain,
that's you, and the breeze
on my cheek in the morning
in the garden, I say,
that is you, too.

And time, that has changed,
or better said, I have changed.
I am not afraid of time now,
I am not running to,
and I am not running from.
You gave me that, and
of course, much else.
But that, that is a lot.

I want you to know, too,
that my context has changed.
The world is my context now.
And also, very important,
when the ghost came,
I didn't run.
I stood steady for you.

Be well,
in every conceivable way.

Mother Superior

In 1954, my parents decided to move from South Bend, Indiana to California, to what would later become known as Wine Country. I was four. I remember leaving, some of the goodbyes, my little brother and I getting into the tan Oldsmobile with the brown roof and setting off west toward the beautiful country.

Our new home was down a dirt road in what had been, until recently, the largest cherry orchard in the world. Large parts of the orchard were still left across the road.

I can remember the biplanes flying over and spraying the trees as we ate breakfast. It was probably DDT, but we didn't think anything of it at the time. We would go out and play in the falling mist with the children of migrant farmworkers who lived across the road.

Sometimes, we would find, in the soil beneath the trees, arrowheads and the bones of the Indians who'd lived there before we did. Behind our new house, the orchards had been scrapped for a golf course and a country club.

About a mile down the dirt road was Falls School, a little one-room schoolhouse with a bell tower that sat beneath a giant black walnut tree. My brother and I and our mother walked to that same corner almost every day to pick up our mail. It was a beautiful country.

I started first grade at Falls. Mrs. White had grades 1-4, and on the other side of the partition, Mr. Mooney had grades 5-8. Maybe about twenty-five kids in total. We sat at our connected desks with the inkwells and the scrolled iron work, and I thought how cramped Loren Lipschitz looked at his desk. He was sixteen and still in the fourth grade. I learned how to read there with Mrs. White, sitting at my desk in the old dark schoolhouse. I had my first fight there, too, under the walnut tree.

Every day, Mrs. White parked her old gray Plymouth in the decrepit teachers' garage. At the end of recess, she would stand on the front steps and ring a handheld bell to signal us to come inside. Sometimes during recess, we would crack open the fallen walnuts and eat them. Once, in the dim, dusty light of the garage, I saw Mrs. White put milk in the radiator of her old gray Plymouth.

About five or six months into the first grade at Falls, my parents thought I would be better off in town at Holy Spirit Catholic School. With another family, we started to carpool over the oak-encrusted hills and through the remaining orchards into town. I had to get a uniform, which was exciting. Charcoal corduroy pants, gray short-sleeve shirt, blue sweater, and black shoes. No exceptions.

I took my seat at the back of the first-grade class at Holy Spirit. Holy Spirit was run by Irish Dominican nuns. They wore black head-covering veils and long, black robes over a white tunic. A rosary as big as a chain and an intimidating thick black belt hung from their waists to their knees.

In second grade, our teacher was a lovely young nun who always seemed a little sad. Once, she went up and down the rows, asking each child if they had a rosary.

"Yes, Sister," I heard all the children say.

Toward the end, when my turn came around, I said I didn't have one, and she walked over to me and handed me a rosary of green beads in a leather case. I have wondered since then whether I really didn't have a rosary or just wanted to see what would happen if I said I didn't. In any event, she died a few weeks later. I would guess now that she was twenty-two or so.

That is when my troubles began. Her replacement was a lay woman, the mother of one of the boys in class. I don't think she liked me. More likely, I'd been unkind to her son, who had a perpetually runny nose.

My attention started to wander, and I began to make frequent trips to the office to see Sister Athanasius, the Mother Superior of Holy Spirit. She was a beautiful, milk-skinned Irish woman with bright-blue eyes, a little older than my mother. She moved briskly down the hallways of Holy Spirit, past the pictures of the saints, with a definitive whoosh of her crisp habit and clicking of her rosary and belt. She and I had very reasonable, even enjoyable talks, and I always got the sense she was smiling at me, that she understood me.

In the third grade, Sister visited one day. My teacher announced in front of the class that, because of lack of effort, I had fallen from the Cardinal reading group to the Bluebird reading group.

Sister looked at me with her eyebrows raised and asked me to stand in front of the class and bend over. She took a yardstick and spanked me, without malice or much force. More like a performance, it seemed to me, for the both of us. I thought it was funny, perhaps even a badge of honor. Some of the kids laughed, too.

Recess at Holy Spirit was an intense affair from start to finish and included fighting and gambling with cards and marbles. I fought nearly every day.

Sister Athanasius kept track of the pandemonium through a picture window in her office. When things got out of hand, she would come on the intercom and yell out, "*Freeze*," in her Irish lilt. Everybody would have to stop dead in their tracks. Sometimes, recess would be called off entirely, or the offenders would have to retire alone to the solitude of their classrooms.

One day in the fourth grade, "*Freeze*" came from the disembodied voice over the intercom, and while struggling to stay motionless in the midst of dragging another boy off the monkey bars, I was summoned to her office.

"Gregory," she said, "how are you? Have a seat."

I took my usual seat.

"I see you fighting almost every day. You're a good fighter," she said. "But I don't think you are very happy here. Do you think you would be happier going back to Falls School?" she asked quietly.

I paused for a moment, understanding clearly for the first time that I would be happier there, that it would be better for me. "Yes, I think I would," I said.

"I could call your father right now, and we can talk to him about it. What do you think?" And then, in much less time than I thought it would take, the three of us were arranging for my immediate return to Falls.

She took my hand into both of her hands as I was leaving and wished me well, smiling at me like a good friend. I never heard another word about it from my father.

The next time I saw her was ten years later during Christmas at Macy's in San Francisco. I had hair below my shoulders and a goatee, was wearing a purple, tie-dye shirt, and was way too high on LSD. I had just brought a ping-pong table for a young kid in the store with

$100 I had in my pocket and had had it sent to his house. I have no idea why.

I walked to the elevator and pressed the down button. The doors opened immediately, and there she was, in all her black-and-white glory. She hadn't seen me in nearly ten years.

"Gregory," she said without missing a beat. "I hope you are behaving yourself? Are you well?"

"Yes, Sister."

"And your mother and father?"

"Yes, they are well,"

"Give them my best," she said. "Merry Christmas, Gregory." She reached out and touched my arm.

"Merry Christmas, Sister," I said. She whooshed past me, and I never saw her again after that.

About thirty years later, my brother called and said he had heard that Sister Athanasius was still alive. She was living in a nursing home for aged nuns somewhere in Los Angeles. He suggested we each write her a letter.

As I wrote mine, she was very vivid to me, and I was happy to tell her she had influenced me, that I had become an educator, too, and as I looked back on it, in no small way because of her. I wanted her to know she had had an impact, and that I was grateful, that my life had turned out in a good way. I sent the letter off and didn't think about it much after.

But about four or five months later, I received a letter from the Mother Superior of the convalescent home. She wanted me to know that my letter arrived the day Sister Athanasius died, that it was read to her by relatives from Ireland who had flown in to be with her, and that, although they couldn't be sure, she seemed to hear my letter and to respond to it. That it was a good thing I had done.

I thought then it was the least I could have done for her, and that the long and lovely arc between us was complete.

The Terme Boxer

You were buried to live,
and you waited, unmoved,
for 2,000 years.
We found you,
brought you up.

We confront you now,
above ground,
face to face,
like the only question
we have ever really had,
the only one we will ever have.

The artist knew your blood
and cast it in copper,
knew our majestic aspirations
and formed it
in scars
and deformations.

The artist knew the song
of your energy, of your defeat,
the song of why, and why
and why, always in repeat,
and it became metallic longing,

as elemental as the moon,
the blood of our
common recognition,
the pulsing of
I can't, but I will.

The pulsing of
I am afraid.
The pulsing of enduring,
of giving pain
and receiving,
of I wonder why,
of I wonder,
of I wonder why

I rise.

The Eremocene

The clear strands of frog eggs wavered
in the flow of the creek water
where the Suisunes drank before me,
where they fished for the steelhead
making their way up from the delta waters,
up through the bear-wandered marshlands,
where the elk drank and grazed
beneath the clouds of duck, geese, and crane.
The grass was still rich for me on the creek
    bank,
the blades tall and sweet at their pale bases.
Some of the eggs had morphed into tadpoles,
and some had become complete in the cycle,
perfectly formed frogs, smaller than acorns.

The world was within me.

I thought that it was mine,
outside of time, of consequence.
I took rocks from the creek bed,
reaching down into the cool water
through the waving strands of green moss.
I lifted up the original power in my hands
and killed the frogs as they scattered
every which way, desperate to live.
Blood stained the water, me, and all around,
bodies ripped, obliterated on the ground.

There was the last one, facing me,
sitting still on a pale white stone.

I sat down, empty, utterly alone.

No angels.
No Christ.
No paradise.

Face to Face with the Butterfly
in the Embrace of the Four Directions

Dear Friends,

I had lunch with my friend Daniel last week. He came straight from his dialysis.

Daniel has a very large and kind face, like a big mountain rounded and softened by time. I could see he wasn't feeling well. He had his left leg amputated last year to save him from diabetes-induced gangrene, but he is getting around pretty well on his prosthesis.

He carries a lot of weight, most of it in his massive upper torso. He is a member of an American southwestern desert tribe, the Tohono O'odham—People of the Desert.

I have looked at lots of late-nineteenth and early-twentieth-century photographs of the O'odham. They were big, strong, vigorous people who had made a rich life in a harsh place—they were some of the fittest people ever to walk the Earth, a race of marathon runners, from the look of the photos.

Among Daniel's ancestors there was no diabetes. That has all changed. Now, over fifty percent of the O'odham have diabetes. Alcoholism is nearly as prevalent. Obesity is the norm.

Millennia of genetic adaptation to the fat and sugar scarcity of the desert and its confrontation with America's fast-and-cheap food cuisine have not been kind to the O'odham.

Daniel gives talks about his people and their land and performs traditional O'odham blessings at various events around town and throughout the state. He wears a red-and-blue velvet stole around his neck when he does them, and he always tells those assembled that he wears it to honor and remember his mother and father. The red, he says, is for his mother, the blue for his father.

He mentioned to me in passing on a couple of occasions that his father was killed in a farm tractor accident when Daniel was a young boy. I had thought that was interesting, because Daniel has gotten involved with a farming cooperative that is trying to grow and reintroduce native foods, so the O'odham can regain their health. I remember thinking his dad would have been proud of that.

During our lunch, Daniel began to talk about his father's death. "You know," he said, "my father was killed on a tractor in the fields."

I said, yes, I knew that, and he went on.

It was in 1959, he said. He was eight years old. His father and mother worked nearly all the time, his father almost always seven days a week. Daniel remembers his mother picking cotton.

The family had literally never gone anywhere as a family. Daniel and his two older sisters, ten and thirteen at the time, had never even been to a zoo or a movie. Then, one morning, Daniel said, his father announced they should all wash and put on their best clothes, because he was going to come home early from work at noon, so he could take them to the Desert Museum.

So, there they were, washed and clean, dressed in the very best they had, waiting to go out on a family outing for the very first time. The anticipation and excitement of it came back into Daniel's face as he spoke to me.

His father didn't arrive at noon, or at one, or at two. Daniel's mother got angry and, by three, was worried. They had no phone, and she didn't know how to drive, so she told her thirteen-year-old daughter, who did know how to drive, to get everyone in the old station wagon and drive them down to the fields, so they could look for him. Daniel was the first to see the tractor from the car.

"It was tipped over, pointing straight up toward the sky," he said. "But I didn't know anything was wrong. I was just excited to find my father. But when I shouted out and pointed toward the tractor, my mother began to cry.

"My sister stopped the car, and I was still excited to see my dad, so I jumped out and ran toward the tractor. Just before I got there, I heard my mother yell out to my sister, 'Grab him!'

"I felt her arm come around me just as I got to the tractor. I remember seeing only my dad's hand, just kind of resting on top of the planer the tractor had been dragging. That's all I remember—his hand coming up and resting there.

"We found out that one of the tractor tires had hit a sinkhole, and when it went in, it threw the tractor backward. I remember there was a lot of oil and battery acid.

"Later that day, after the ambulance came, the tow truck came to get the tractor and towed it by our house. The steering wheel was all bent, and there was oil and battery acid down the sides of the tractor. My mom said he was still alive when we got there, but I don't know. We don't know how long he was there."

I don't know why Daniel told me his story. Certainly, there wasn't a trace of self-pity. He just seemed to want me to know about that part of his life. But the image of him and his sisters and mother, dressed in their best and waiting for his father to come home, struck me and stayed with me like a dream.

I looked into his face and thought that all of us, at some time in our lives, if just for a moment, are washed, dressed in our best, and waiting with the certain expectation that our deepest hopes will be fulfilled.

When I was about five or six, I was playing with a friend in a small ditch at the side of a road. The ditch was overgrown with mustard and wheat grass beneath a row of black walnut trees that had just leafed out. Walnut husks were fermenting on the ground, and the sunlight was falling through just here and there in dapples of light. We were engulfed in the vegetation, some of it as high as our heads.

Suddenly, an iridescent yellow-and-black butterfly the size of my head arose very slowly and suspended itself right in front of my face. I was struck, mystified. It had stopped me, taken me either far outside of myself or deeper into myself, I still can't decide which. I have been stopped that way since but never again quite so completely or vividly. It was my first remembered encounter with a world that might exist whether I was in it or not.

Daniel's story about his father stopped me, too. Only this time, I had adult questions: Why is it we have to suffer like that? Why would Daniel's father die beneath a tractor on the one day he had set aside for his family? Is it all just happenstance, some of it more resonant than the rest?

Daniel's story about his father was essential to who he is. My story of being stopped by the butterfly is essential to who I am. We tell a story to ourselves about who we are, for good, for bad, and in between, and then we work it out in the world.

Being eaten by a lion would be a powerful story but a horrible end. But we know about that story deep-down, and we are terrified. The lion is coming. Daniel's father is not. We long to know why, and we long for there to be a purpose to it all. Our longing and our fear unite us. No matter how proud, how different, or indifferent (indifference is a kind of suffering, too) we appear to be, we are being washed up and formed against one another by our shared fears and our shared sorrow.

Our lives pass away quickly as-fireflies in the dark. Some of us are healthy, some not. Some educated, some not. Some wise, some unwise. Some have had two loving parents and a home with food, laughter, and support; some have had nothing, maybe worse than nothing. Some walk with confidence and certainty, others with trembling and fear. Each of our stories is unique in its particulars. Daniel's father died in his own unique way; a butterfly startled me in its own unique way. But the veil of differences that separates us is thin. Every story could be our own.

Daniel had plenty of cause in his life for bitterness and despair. He is a member of a nation that has unjustly lost most of its ancestral lands and whose people were nearly destroyed by the civilization that overran them and whose ways continue to injure them. His losses were harsh, and sometimes, he is considered to be a foreigner or an oddity, a remnant, in his own land.

Yet, he is a healer. He is sought after to give traditional blessings at many public functions, some for just a few, others for thousands. And he is remarkably the same at each. He carefully puts on his red-and-blue stole, speaks of his mother and father and the Earth, addresses the "Creator God" in both Tohono O'odham and English, raises the eagle feathers in his right hand, and then asks everyone to turn with him to the four directions, asking for grace and blessings upon all the people assembled and upon the Earth itself. Even excited crowds become silent during those moments as they turn to the four directions.

Daniel seems to break some kind of spell at the blessings, and, at least when I'm there, the biggest story seems to be that we are on this Earth at all. There is something fundamentally powerful about being in a group as it turns silently to the four directions and, at least for a while, those who are there appear to remember this.

Daniel could have chosen a life of despair. Many who have experienced similar circumstances have. He tells a different story.

It is easy to forget that we are deeply connected to others and to the world around us and that our actions resonate in ways we may not understand. When Daniel raises the eagle feathers, I remember the butterfly. It seems, at that moment, face to face with the butterfly and in the embrace of the four directions, we remember the world and the world remembers us.

Ahora, El Tiempo Me Mira

Time watches me now,
like an old friend.
Get down on the ground
before the flowers, she says,
yet again,
put your forehead
to the damp ground
beneath the clearing night sky,
so that the dirt of the
incomprehensible ages clings
to your forehead, reaching for you,
breathe in the smell
of the incomprehensible earth
and of the flowers,
yet again,
the stars and the universes
above and all around.
You will not go away.

Or, sit up straight
for your people,
for those who carried you here,
for those who will carry you away,
for those ripped up
as trees can be ripped
out of the earth
by machines,
for those put in cages,
for the children
who are shot
as they reach
for bread
in a world where everything
is known
and nothing is understood.
Sit up straight for your people.
Stand straight for your people
until you might stand no more,
then fall to the ground,
be with your people there.

Or, distracted, the sun,
down west at the horizon,
startles you, last light of day,
within the vestigial clouds
of rain, the sky nacreous,
iridescent as an abalone shell
tilted to the light,
understand that this is her,
in your heart, this is your heart,
untouchable, this is
your decision,
and so it will be.

Time watches me now.
Open yourself to the worlds.
Be straight for your people.
Weep, but fear nothing,
she says.

The Vishnu Layer

Not exactly,
not exactly a dream,
finding you wandering
in the dark, in the hallway,
wondering where
you were, wondering.

I bowed so as not
to startle you, but
you were not startled.
I embraced you,
finding you again,
fitted, complete.

I led you to our bed
and we lay down,
to comfort
one another there,
in that place
that no one but you and I
have ever known

throughout all of time
in all of the universes,
enough time to see
the Vishnu Layer
turn to sand
and back again,
just you and me
there
in that place
where no one else
has ever been
or ever will,

then you looked
at something behind me,
something I couldn't see,
and you went there easy,
and that was our peace.

Maybe I will join you there,
maybe I will one day,
if what you saw
becomes mine, too,
to see.

And That Was It, Babe

I am laid out on the couch,

the couch where

you used to be,

next to the flowers

and the candle

burning for you,

the couch across

from my chair,

the noon winter sun

all across my face,

and I am thinking

there is only

ever one thing

happening in the moments

of this world,

but we are mostly

too small, or too busy

or too distressed, too hurt,

too frightened to see it.

All that.

The warmth of the winter
sun on the couch soothes me,
feels like it is penetrating
my body, all the hurt places.
The warmth I felt when
I placed you
in the crematorium
was an awakening,
when I went as far
as I could, baby,
though in the revelation
of that final warmth
as I rolled you away deeper
into the fire
I understood in the contemplative
bones of the body
and the heat-cleared labyrinths
and caverns of the mind
that I could say that we,
that we had done
what we set out to do,
wrap it up together
just like always, you and me,
that I could walk into
the fire with you
and be at peace,
be at peace
in what we lived and did,
goodbye, and complete.

I had a dream, baby.
I was in the body
of life itself,
in the living aggregation
of connection, arteries
veins and nerves
and connective tissues
otherworldly and of all sorts
running in all 10,000 directions,
and at first, I was afraid,
expecting to be feel trapped
in something foreign,
but I felt space and release instead,
at the center of the universe,
and my face and body
relaxed into ease and recognition,
just like yours did
when you awakened and were frightened
to see me, but then you saw me
and reached out the last time for me,
put your arms around me,
told me you loved me.

And that was it, babe.

That was the dream.

Thanksgiving

Standing here in the middle of the world,
as I am
on this day of thanksgiving
with the food spread out before us
in the light of the candles
we have placed and lit
along these long tables,
lit so that the light itself
coruscates from our eyes
and over the food itself
and reflects in the wine
and in the water, itself,
as we sit beside one another
not sure where the light and food begin
and where we end,
I see it is no small thing to be seated here
in the mist of our evanescing and mingling breath,
here in our wondrous agitation.
Let it become a memory
that soothes us and assures us,

even when we can no longer remember.
Standing here in the middle of the world,
as I am
on this day of thanksgiving,
I think that there is something in us,
that is not us,
that it is the best of us.
I cannot name it,
but I raise my glass of wine
dark as a plum skin bruise,
raise it to you
knowing that we all know full well
that there is deep injury here
as in a tree that has splintered
and is bleeding amber sap,
half itself ripped away by the wind,
gnarling at night in the moonlight,
flinching but accommodated to the sun,
knowing full well as we do,
as I was saying,
that my beloved and your true friend,
our light stopped here for a while,
is gone, here only in the spirit of our assembly,
and that at a time not too distant,
we will put her ashes in black marble
and take them out to the cirrus flowers
that surround
to bury them there
in the loving ground.

Yes, standing here as I am,

in the center of the world,

I can see that there has been

a change, a new season,

that sitting here beside one another

is no distraction, but a communion

of surrendered startlement,

a comfort of recognition, of affection.

Did you know that a grove of trees

can sense the injury of one of its fellows,

and that they will send nutrients through their

    roots

and their home biome to their injured other?

I raise my glass to you and to that,

and to all that we do not know or understand,

I raise my glass to the man who lost

his wife and children and twenty-two of his family

    members

and who is living in the rubble of his former home

in the cold and dripping rain,

I raise my glass to all

that we do not understand

and to the light of his candle.

I raise my glass to you,

And I bleed.

South Station, Boston

September, 2025

When my first flight out of Boston to D.C. was cancelled due to weather, I received a text indicating that I had been booked on the next departing flight, five hours later at 8:00 p.m. I was sitting next to a black woman named Stephanie, with long blonde dreadlocks, who was heading to Cleveland on a flight that had been delayed. I thought I might go look for something to eat down the concourse and asked Stephanie if she would mind watching my backpack for a few minutes.

There were a lot of people who had their own troubles, working their phones trying to make other arrangements. I passed on the fast-food places and walked into something called the Country Marketplace.

There were several tiers of sandwiches in a refrigerated case. They looked good. I normally wouldn't buy a sandwich from a refrigerated case, but the day had been long and promised to get longer. I looked at a handsome ham and cheese. I probably wouldn't get that, but I could see it as a possibility, if the day grew longer. The price tag at the bottom of the sandwich said $17.25 in bold black. I took a photo of it to send to friends. I put it back on its shelf carefully and settled for a small, five-dollar coffee.

When the young Latina woman behind the counter took my money, I mentioned the sandwich. She gave me a look, just a hair's breadth short of a small smile, to say that, yes, it was outrageous, but clearly she was used to shock of it. The sandwich was probably approaching two times her hourly pay.

I showed the sandwich photo to Stephanie. She laughed outright.

Turns out Stephanie, five foot two or three, at best, was returning from a trip to Bali with her friend, Michelle. They had been in transit for over twenty-four hours.

It was a warmup for her retirement, she said. She was retiring in January from a twenty-six-year career as a police officer in Cleveland. She showed me photos of Bali, including one of her in a flowing, yellow, angel-like gown that was included for use in the ticket price for being pushed out high over a lush rain forest on a giant swing. Though I couldn't see it, she assured me she was tied in securely.

Later, she showed me photos of her four sons and her grandchildren, including one of her children with her eighty-two-year-old father on his thirty acres in Alabama that had been in the family for over a hundred and twenty years, and that had been illegally seized at some point then regained with great effort and diligence. Her father was half Creek, she said.

When Stephanie and Michelle, with her six-foot-long rolled-up painting from Bali that reminded her of a Basquiat, got up to go, I thought to myself that flying over the rain forest in flowing gowns was just right for them.

As they walked away, I got another text. My 8:00 p.m. flight was cancelled, and there were no other flights leaving until the next day. Those, as I soon discovered, were full, with standby only, in some cases a dozen or so people deep.

My half-sister, whom I hadn't seen for eight years, was expecting me in Arlington the next morning for the only day we had available to spend together. I needed to be there. I wanted to be there and was intent on being there.

I had been looking at train costs, and they seemed to be rising by the minute. What had been a $200 ticket appeared to rise in minutes to $500. I was standing in line to talk to a ticket agent about flight options when I saw and overheard an older man and his wife desperately trying to secure a hotel room. They didn't look particularly experienced at maneuvering under these circumstances, but I heard him say into his phone excitedly that, yes, they would take the room available.

The next thing I heard him say was, "$750?" He repeated it. "*$750? For one night?*"

"That's not what it was," I heard him say, his wife sitting beside him, her pale eyes darting back and forth to him and something in the distance and her hands poised to grab the phone from her husband, but she let him finish. It seemed to me they'd taken the room. I wanted to ask, but I didn't. I realized then, standing beside them, that our misery is being mined by the algorithms.

When I got to the ticketing desk, I was greeted by a tall, dignified young man in a coat and matching vest who appeared to be from India. The only sign that he had been dealing with frustrated and panicked people for hours was a slightly askew tie. He took in my details, issued me a refund, and said, in essence, this is not going to get any better.

"Go to the front of the terminal, take the shuttle to South Station, and catch a bus to Washington. It's your best option. I hope things work out for you."

I bought a bus ticket online. In fact, I bought two, so I would have some room, justifying to myself that it was still just half of the what the plane had cost. Then, I headed for the Boston South Station shuttle. I missed the first one, not realizing that the one loading up right in front of me was the one I was looking for, so I had to wait another twenty minutes in the rain.

When it came, without realizing it, I sat down in a row reserved for seniors and the disabled. Straight across from me sat a woman who appeared to be in her eighties. With her long, white, healthy-looking hair in pigtails, she was dressed all in white, over which she wore a transparent rain slicker. The only color she wore was on thick, striped, green-and-black socks in new-looking black flats with a strap and buckle. She was immaculate, the tiny royal crone of Oz, with a kind face and a direct, untroubled gaze. She had a wisp of white hairs on her chin, and beside her was an enormous piece of black luggage with wheels, also covered in plastic to keep it dry. On top of that lay a very large blue Walmart bag, all of it carefully arranged.

She looked up at me from her stooped sitting position and smiled. "Are you coming home?" she asked in a genteel but unaffected sort of way.

"No," I said. "I'm on my way to Washington."

"Oh," she said. "Well, next time, there is a very nice beach here to walk on. You could try it."

"Yes," I said. "And you, where are you headed?"

"Yes," she said, "that is always the question, isn't it?"

As we came to her stop, my first inclination was to help her with that enormous case and bag, but before I could get up, stooped as she was, she manhandled them off the bus and moved them expertly over to a wall out of the rain, as if she had been doing it for a very long time. As the shuttle pulled away, it occurred to me she was going to be getting on the next shuttle because she had no other place to go.

The shuttle descended down an incline into the underworld of South Station, a place of contradictory signs and stairways leading to nowhere or the wrong there, a place of twilight and empty, unadorned spaces built for busy stadium-like crowds of people. Even the occasional person who seemed to work somewhere within the space wasn't sure where the bus terminal was.

I bought a bag of peanuts from an Arab man who had a little snack cart on wheels next to a mysterious escalator. A young White man about thirty, wearing stained clothing, came up and asked if he could buy a $2.00 soda for a dollar. The vendor thanked me and wished me well.

I entered another space, a circular room lined with empty ticketing counters. I asked a man in a security uniform leaning against a pillar if he knew where the buses loaded up. He appeared to try to speak but ended up just gesturing with his hand for me to continue walking in a general direction.

I did that, but found nothing but another nearly empty, high-ceilinged cavern of a room. I went back to the circular room. The security guard was still at his pillar and looked at me, seemingly apologetically, but said nothing.

I found a man sitting at a ticketing booth with the light on, and he said that often the bus schedules aren't posted, but that, yes, the security guard had been right. So, I couldn't be sure, but my bus would depart from the room that the guard had directed me to, from either gate 8 or 9.

My wife of fifty-three years, Vicki, died eight months ago as of this writing, on January 16, 2025. Our sons and I were on our knees at her side when life left her eyes.

The twilight emptiness of the interior of South Station seemed familiar to me, a manifestation of aspects of my interior life since her death. I loved her with all my heart. I am still learning what it means to love with all your heart. A few days earlier, before arriving at South Station, I had been standing at sunrise on the beach of Gabarus, a small fishing village on the southeastern coast of Cape Breton, Nova Scotia, where I was visiting Claire, my friend and witness.

I walked the beach with Vicki there. Walked within the sound of the waves and stones, as they rattled like seeds with the ebb and flow. Watched the sun rise over the unobstructed Atlantic with her, selected the stones that she would like, so we could keep this memory and hold them in our hands in another place. We were enveloped, the water, the rolling stones, motion itself, the light coming straight to us over the sea as it does. Enveloped by our life together, the sea, and Vicki and the stones and their soft rattling, the ebb and flow, the unimaginable spin of the Earth, which also turns within us, all come to a still point, and we all wept there as one, the light, the motion, the stones, Vicki and I, our life together, for what was lost and for what was gained.

There was a young Black couple at Gate 8 with a boy about three, sitting on his mother's lap. They were unsure as I was whether we were in the right place or not, and the young man, standing in front of his wife and child, kept examining the worn paper itinerary he held in his hand. He was dressed in shorts and a T-shirt, and the young mother sitting beside me was tall and very thin, like a certain type of elegant model. She wore a dark, flower-patterned, short-sleeve shirt, dark pants, and a head scarf.

We spoke a little, and the little boy, still waking up from sleep in his mother's lap, kept looking at the peanuts in my hand. I offered him some, but he didn't react. He kept looking. His mother asked him if he wanted some, and she helped him hold out his hand so I could pour out some for him. She asked me where I was headed, and I said Washington. She said they were going to Birmingham, Alabama.

"Have you ever been to Birmingham?" she asked in a sing-song way that suggested, if I hadn't been, I should go.

"No, I haven't. How long will that take?" I asked her.

"Two and a half days."

I got up to go to the restroom, and the young man told me that it was at the far end of the circular room, maybe 150 yards back where we had come from. A few minutes later, while I was waiting for a $2.60 bottle of water at a tiny, six-foot-long McDonald's counter with a battery of computerized ordering menus, I felt a tap on my shoulder. It was the young man, breathing hard. He had run up to tell me that the bus had arrived, and then he turned and ran back toward the gate and his family.

More people had arrived at the gate, but the young couple were standing to the side as others were checked in by the driver. The young man still held onto their tattered itinerary. They didn't have any luggage, just a small tote bag. I wondered if they had money for food for their long journey to Birmingham.

The Black driver clearly did not want to be there. I heard him thinking, *Who is this old, White man in the Indiana Jones hat, getting on this bus with all these invisibles in the dead of night?* That's what was in his eyes. God knows what burdens he was carrying.

I showed him the digital ticket on my phone for my two seats, 4C and 4D, and got on the bus. I found a young couple in their mid-teens, seventeen at best, in the seats I had purchased. They were dressed in pajamas, enraptured in each other, holding onto each other tightly and happily, with a blanket around them.

The boy, for he really was a boy, showed me his tickets for 4C and 4D. They had been sold twice. Better to stand or sit on the floor, I thought, than hassle these children. I found a seat across the aisle.

My people from Birmingham were the last people on the bus, itinerary tight in hand. After they walked by me, making their way to the back of the bus, I never saw them again, but I thought I heard the boy crying a little bit here and there during the night, and I wished I had given him more of my peanuts. All of my peanuts.

Nothing worked on the bus. Not the overhead lights, not the charging outlets, not the much-touted Internet. I saw people try to charge their phones and turn on the overhead lights, then inevitably unplug their charging cords. No one did that in frustration, but rather with resignation. No one, it seemed, had really expected any of it to work, and they sat back to try to get some sleep.

Whenever we stopped during the night, the overhead lights would come on and some people would get on and some would get off. In New York, the boy and girl in 4C and 4D got off, carrying their blanket, and I moved over to their seats.

In Newark, a young couple got on. The young man told me I was in their seats and showed me his tickets. 4C and 4D had been sold a third time. They took seats across the aisle and one row up. I reached across the aisle to show him my tickets.

"I got you," he said. When I turned back around in the lights, I saw a beautiful young woman with long, black hair who was dressed all in white with a very low-cut sports bra. Our eyes met, and we both smiled briefly. That was the only smile I saw on the bus.

She got off in Philadelphia into a street scene that seemed to be happening at all of the stops, with people sleeping under old blankets in the littered streets, others milling about in the back alleys and hidden spaces that all big cities have. The incredible woman in all white could have been a dancer or a track athlete. She stood with a friend and took a tiny dog out of her purse, lit a cigarette, and seemed to be enjoying a triumphant return home. I couldn't be sure, but I think she was a trans woman. What does it matter? It was the only smile I had had all night.

As we pulled out, the Black man across the aisle from me got up and sat in the two empty seats in front of me. He was about sixty, lean with close cropped hair, dressed entirely in black from his black hoodie to his shined black shoes. His pants had a black velvet stripe down the leg, like old tuxedo pants. He had been sitting up straight as an arrow for hours, still and looking quietly ahead. When he sat down in front of me, he put the hood of his jacket over his head and leaned way back into his seat.

I did make it to see my sister. My dad left her and her brother with their mother in Detroit when they were ten and five, respectively. That wound was enormous, a wound that probably never closes, but I wouldn't know definitively, because it didn't happen to me. I have never tried to defend what he did, but I know it troubled him until he died.

My sister, Susan and I had a wonderful visit. We have always enjoyed each other. When the time came to say goodbye, I embraced her and began to move toward the door. And then, I reached back and embraced her again, harder, closer, longer. I was back at the sea, the sunrise, the rattling stones, the still point with Vicki.

"That one is from your father," I said.

Slight Air

I know what beauty
    is now
that's what I thought
when the sunset
caught me by surprise
    last night
and you were there
    with me
like now when
the first of the
summer rain
    is falling
and you are here
    with me
watching and listening
    the thunder
I know what
    it is now

I know what happened
            entangled,
            integrated,
what I hear
            you hear
what I see
            you see
the cool rain air on
            my face
slips across yours
the rain is you
the rain is me
the sunset was you
the sunset was me
the rain falling
the rain falling

I know what
you want me to do—
I always did
I did it for you

If my last thought
is of going
      to you
it will be done
what we set out
      to do
and we will now
      move through
the worlds dying
and the worlds
      becoming
as slight air
through the
      high grass.

At the Altar of Being

The sphinx moths are large,
the size of a delicate hand, say,
my wife's hand,
the wings black and white
in fractal repetitions,
their eyes aglow in the dark
when struck by light, like a deer,
a dozen of them in amongst
the midnight cereus blooms
glowing white, there is nothing whiter
than the desert night flowers,
which spend just one night
under the moonlight
in the moist, cinnamon-scented air,
the sound of sphinx moths'
slowly undulating wings
the only sound there is,
then the graceful dropping descent
between the velvet, long-expectant petals,

through the powdery mist
of the anther's saffron pollen
as the long tongue unfolds
and slips between the labia
of the stigma and the stamens
and laps at the sweet nectary.

I think I should pray here,
that if I am to be left behind,
it would be good to pray,
to get down on a knee,
but one knee is not enough,
to get down on both knees
in the gravel and the dirt
here amongst the sphinx moths
and the cereus blooms in
the perfumed moonlit air
is to relinquish any claim
other than to being,
to be suspended between
ineffable grief and
ineffable gratitude, to be
both those in the instant,
to let the heart grow larger
than can be imagined

at the altar of these beings,
of this being.
This is all there ever really was,
all that there really is,
all we ever need or needed.

I read of the last man
of an uncontacted tribe
deep in the Amazon, alone
and hidden for thirty years
from those who destroyed

all that he loved and knew
and understood,

from those who wanted
more than there is.
They found him dead
in his hammock
outside of his hut,
adorned in a rainbow
of macaw feathers,
ready at last
for the moment
when he could
fly to his people.

I understand him
here, with the flowers,
the moths, the moon,
the sound of the
undulating fractal wings.
with this gift of air,
he is my brother,
he is our brother,
and I, too,
and we, too,
when left behind,
adorned in feathers,
will fly
to our people.

Bound

We are light, stopped
for a while,
layered like the canyons,
broken and formed
by compressions
and violent exposures,
the salted striations of
famine and fine meat,

laid down in
discernable patterns,
the geology of consciousness,
every breath a descent
and an ascent
through the strands
of loss, of consummation
on the brilliant stone,
the waste of days,

the suspension of
pearlescent understandings,
the original
fidgeting bewilderment
that built the cities,
pulls the trigger.

One light year, or
thirteen billion,
it's all the same
for us.

We as we are
won't be traveling
either distance.
We are stopped here,
in the fragile bright,
stranded in the badlands
and in the goodlands,
abandoned, beyond brave,
outraged,
gnawing blind
on the foundations,
our devices
unequal yet
to the origins of

our unbound love.

Grace

Reality lives in bread.
All the world is there,
the past, the present,
and the future, in its lair.

The rain is there,
that fell on the grain,
the hands and the labor,
machines born from brain.

The heat and the light
that wakened the wheat,
cloud, sky, sun, and river
made it ready to eat,

The yeast is there
half a billion years,
alive, come down from
who knows where?

The salt we crave,
seed of wars, cities, dread,
traded for children and slaves.
All there. Smell of bread.
The minerals, the remains,
up through the stems,
mothers, all the world contains,
to our mouths and out again.
The crazy prophets, the first
to put water and grain to fire,
all those who have known desire,
relentless procession, best to worst.

The ones who don't have it,
can smell it but not eat,
their meal of desolation
washes down, becomes our defeat.

Unbroken staff of life,
gift of conditions that are just right,
all we contain, peace and strife,
remind us with life and loving sight.

False Coordinates

I love you all,

want you desperately,

but you cannot be

my coordinates.

I can't set my

way by you,

by what you say,

by your attention,

your tribute,

your disdain,

your adulation

or your pain.

If I am in a dream,

in the womb of a sycamore

above the water

of a sacred river

on the edge

of a pristine frozen plain,

that's my business,

mine alone.

I can't have
you doing the calculations
for a way through
that you can't see
and that only
I can follow, can I?

(When I say, "I,"
think, "you.")

If you don't like
the color of my shirt,
or the part in my hair,

should I pretend
I'm not alone and
brush it over

the other way
so that you'll

be happy
and someday
I'll be sad?

No, the truth
is, everyone
is already in
the rearview mirror
and I am going
directly to
the place that
only
I can know.

You, too.

Impervious

"Consider your final hours."

—Marcus Aurelius circa, 180 C.E.

In the pure dark,
no noise or sparkle,
pray that memory
of you in four hundred
or four thousand years
comes as a kindred and fair touch.
You, unnamed but not disguised,
carried like a flower on clear water
across the evanescent generations,
unbidden, royal, impervious
to the blind swirl of chaos.

Last Day on Earth

Oh my God,
Look at that tomato.
Red. So red.
The glistening geometry
of the interior,
the deep genealogy
of the seeds
expressed through time.
Nightshade of the Americas.

A fruit, a pod containing seed,
conceived in the ovary,
which reminds me
of the burgundy cherries,
the orchard
where my mother and I walked,
the burgundy, the silvery bark,
the light falling through the leaves
rustling in the sudden
warm breeze,
the soft overturned dirt.

My mother, lovely,
troubled person
that she was,
could see beauty,
but was wary
of receiving it.

I was with her
on her last day,

at her last moment.

It had always been
right there, the beauty,
the fruit just right
there for the taking.

A hard thing for her
to see at the end.

I wrapped her in
a shroud, kissed
her smooth forehead,
took her to the hearse.
Please respect her
in every possible way,
I said, and walked
away in the dappled
light beneath the trees.

Veteran's Day

Out kneeling beside the small garden plot,
no bigger than a round table for two,
in the quiet of the afternoon, not knowing
quite what to do, desperate,
ancient terrors arising in the body,
thinning the radishes,
which don't look like they will ever develop,
the greens too tall, reaching too hard for
the scant sun with nothing left for the
center.

On my knees
there beside the essential
simplicities, there with me all of the myth-
making, the ennobling incantations,
no brother or sister left behind,
the cause greater than self makes a self,

and the nineteen-year-old veteran
who lost two legs, two arms, two ears, and
two eyelids to burning scythes of copper,
(an IED, a Humvee),
torso bolted
to the bed, shrouded in hissing mists to
cool his carbonized skin,
unblinking eyes covered with
moisturizing goggles.
Let him go.
What have we done?
What are we?
Where do we come from?
Rising up on two legs two million
years ago
to here. To here.

The spinach is coming in slow,
too, probably won't get above six inches.

I knew exactly what it was
when I heard it, my head down
beside the garden,
a hummingbird, and I knew
when I looked up
it would be there,

two feet up above to the right,
silhouetted, suspended in the twigs,
there, just like the tree was there
in the battle photograph
of the dying soldier, and I wondered
as he lay dying if maybe he didn't
reach out to touch it,
to thank it for being there,
something alive and less complicated,
something not fierce or hungry,
a quiet, grateful recognition,
and I was not surprised at all
that the hummingbird
had come
and saved
my
life.

Diggers

We slipped into your graves, screaming
Little boys hungry with treasure;
Bones, beads, perfect teeth.

Not many of you were complete,
but one was surrounded by elk bones
We brushed the moist black soil from you.
Stood above you looking down quietly and not
    knowing why.

Rich, four eyes, he cracked your skull
into little slivers with a lead pipe.
The formation dissolved before our faces. No
    one moved.

My mother did not like your teeth
in the house. Arrowheads were all right.
So were two stones that fit together, metates,
for crushing acorns. Everybody likes your
    metates.

Your teeth I hid in the ivy.
After school we looked and looked,
but we never did see you there in the teeth.

The ground was going bare, scholarly diggers put
     up ropes,
caught us up short running, stay away do not
     touch,
big trucks took your village to a room in the
     museum.

Someone stole your teeth, my teeth, from the
     ivy.
All my arrowheads went somewhere like the
     years did.
I sold the metates for movie money.

You were forgotten, until I came running
     through the hills,
fell, reached out, and felt your cold knife.
Long deep black, shining obsidian, jagged on two
     sides sharper than steel.
I saw you there, in the knife, beneath the oak.
I did not take it home.

Enough

I am the shadow of a bird
flying overhead, unseen,
but in my mind, winging
inexorably to paradise.

No one will remember
our names, and even
if some do, not for long,
they will just be names.

Yet there we are on the lilac
Hillside, picking oranges, your eyelashes
on my cheek like the feet of a bee
with nothing left to prove, in eternity.

How to give thanks for that?
Beneath a tree swaying in easy wind,
that's where I would like to die,
saying this is what I am.

A creature among creatures,
undeserving, but not to blame,
unleashed from misinterpretation,
no need for courage or a story.

Coffee with a friend,
the sound of a chime,
a reunited brother's gift of bread,
as they are forever, in time.

How could I ask for more?
Consuming leaves me empty.
In the shadow of a passing bird,
unseen, I am enough.

Identity

Two birds,
out the window
in the tree.

What is reality?

They jump
from branch
to branch,
enraptured,
entangled,
lives to live,
like you
and me.

Velvet new growth
quivers beneath
their activity.
Time contains us,
we contain time,
within the still totality.

Faith

Sometimes the obsidian heart
reveals itself, displaces all
other considerations
and potentialities with
its broken, chipped,
tendon-cutting edges,
the blackest of all
clarities, black, black,
black. The blackest
and most beautiful
of all certainties
that cannot be worn away,
evaded,
insistent as the sun.

I fell once, alone,
a child, but the man coming
close from within,
in a meadow

beneath a mother oak
in California, not far
from the inland encroachments
of the sea,
an oak rooted deep, insistent,
indomitable until it
can or could not be,
It had fed
many creatures
before me.

I fell,
put my hand out,
felt the cold hard black
of an obsidian spearhead, larger
more elegant, say, than my foot.
It entered right there,
has never
let me go,
has shaped me in life
and in death
with its implacable, black certitude.

Ancestors' Chant

Consider this.

We cried, failed,
succeeded, fucked,
shat, and stole.
Worked in the dirt,
shivered, sweat,
and shook, studied,
tossed and turned,
got up with the sun,
slept late and drunk,
smelled the new spring,
had our hopes, dreams,
prayed, got sick, and died.
Drifted night and day
in unbearable loss,
bore the loss,
looked at the same stars
you look at,
wondered why,

sent ourselves
to you
through the doors
of your body,
your ears and eyes,
your truth,
your crooked smile,
your raised eyebrow,
your special tic,
your special inclinations,
your bad teeth,

your good teeth,
your crooked view.

We dazzled
and we disappointed,
we laughed, we wailed,
we betrayed

and we stayed,
we whistled and wept,
blundered and thundered,
multiplied, divided,
gutted and strutted,
hid and undid,
deceived and believed,
sniveled and wheedled,
lied and cheated,

lived well, created hell,
gave and split apart,
lost and found
our hearts,
again and again.

This is your patrimony,
your inheritance,
and we are all
counting on you,
putting our money
and our final breaths on you.
Stand straight, for Christ's sake,
see what we didn't see,
become what we
wanted to be,
walk on the blessed planet
like a
goddamn noble,
love, fear nothing,
love again, and again,
set yourself free.
All of us who came,
all of us who are coming,
we'll be in you,
behind you,
right beside you,
all around you,
just like we've always been.

El Cuerpo

-Canto Primero-
El Serpiente y Cadenas

The body says hello,
greets us, is hospitable,
exacting, a familiar stranger
with expectations,
requirements,
unceasing demands,
gifts, secret powers, rooms,
chambers where it stores
various odds and ends,
like the snake,
like the snake that
hissed and darted,
startled me, in shorty pants,
hand in soft hand
with the mother,
on our way to the church,

the dark, cool church,
where men in white
and golden robes
swung balls breathing
sweet smoke
from rattling chains
and spoke words
I didn't know,
still don't' know,

the snake hissed
and darted on the left,
l lunged from my mother,
or was it for my mother,
lunged for security,
the world, I see,
is not as I wish it to be,
the great emptiness
of terror constricted
my throat
taunted and pressed
the small
strong heart.

The body
never forgets,
all of it
in the special chambers
and places,
so it will know,
I suppose,
how to conjure
terror whenever
and wherever
it pleases

and the rattling chains
of the censers
became the snakes
of my back,
the constrictors
of my throat
that stretch
and contract
and go slack
as they are wont
to do
when they do
because the body time
is a different time,

the snake entered
forever as the body is,
still there,
the snake in the body.
Strange.
Strange that the body,
gift of time,
giver of time,
strange that the body
can't keep better time.

May as well be yesterday
or today or seventy years on,
all that the body retains,
the chains wrapped
uptight around terror,
the sudden empty of the snake,
the soft hand gone,
the sweet smoke rising
to heaven as
a frightened prayer.

Full of Grace

The end is in the beginning,
in the blood, the gristle
and the bone.

What we do wears us down,
what we don't do
wears us down, too.

We are a tangle,
neurons, passionate replication,
entangled, a longing expression.

Our sameness
is in our strangeness,
our shared arrival here.

The earth breathes
itself through our bodies,
pleads for us to live.

The arc of innocence
is long, tattered,
it passes through despair.

We can say again and again
don't ever leave me,
but it is already done.

In silence and emptiness
we tremble and shake,
we cry out, cry out and fall.

Prone before the universes,
the breaths of 1,000 Buddhas
sweep over the ravines of our hearts.
La Virgen whispers
the sweet weeping of being
into our seashell ears.

If not those, then, for you,
in the blood, gristle, and bone,
we are a finality and not alone.

Dear Friend

You want to know about
storms, and I write now
to ask which ones I
should write about.

The storm of desire
sweeping me up in
the kaleidoscope tide of fire,
compressing body and mind
to spear the purpose,
char the emptiness?

The storm of despair,
stirring in the core,
sweeping to the heart,
to the brain to make lead
and the dull murmurs of wind,
the world is lost, is lost?

The storm of acts done
and undone, regrets,
murders, dreams of murders
betrayals, dreams of betrayals,
the sad, stone conclusion,
I'm no good, never been no good?
The storm of realization,
of a banal, phony nation,
never what it claimed to be,
lurching in surprised decline
toward its shrouded destiny
of decay and reckoning?

The midnight storm of fear,
of the heart beating,
waiting for the predator,
for the terrible blood end,
the teeth deep in my throat
ripping everything away?

The storm of not right, crazy,
half-awake imaginings,
blank-eyed human fish
crowded into receding seas,
their horrors and deeds now
incomprehensible jabberings?

In any event, let me know
which one intrigues you,
if any at all,
and I'll do my best.

Morning Time

Our bodies entwined,
washed by the falling cool air,
doves out on the line,
doing what doves do
in the summer morning time.
My face buried in your hair,
smell of coconut, so fine.

I still see the stars there.

Down

Yes, I want to be held.
I am beat, down, fallen.
I think I am defeated.

I can barely look up from
this hard, uneven ground,
but I can see the world,
I love the world,
have always loved the world,
the leaves moving
in the air, or waving,
as they did when I was a child,
I love even the myriad of hot,
sharp stones under my weight
pressing into my chest and abdomen,
I love the birds speaking back to the chimes
that my people have hung around,

yet, I am down,
I can't raise my hand
or a finger to erase
the dry, rich mica-sparkled
dust from my surrendered lips,
lips bequeathed by
my mother and father,
and their mothers and fathers,
and theirs, and theirs.

Thank you for these lips,
it occurs to me,
for these lips, for these teeth
like bone,
hard-pressed now,
finally melding
what belongs to the earth.

The body told me again and again
that this day would come,
and now all of it hurts,
my hair is tired, even though
it rustles a bit in the wind
like the leaves, saying hello,
(or perhaps that movement is a bug)

here we are splayed out
on the sharp ground,
heat of the sun on my
back through my ripped shirt,
the day has come.

Just because I'm leaving it
doesn't mean I don't love it,
does it, here in stilled rebellion,
a contrition, a submission
on this vast plain of miraculous stone,
vast plain of sky, blood, sinew,
my lover's lips soft on my burning ear,
yes you are down,
she breathes the sound
that travels to me
like my first
uncorrupted breath,
yes you are down
she breathes the sound,
her fingers glide down
my stained cheek
like a mist of golden pollen,

yes you are down, fallen, finished,
breath of pollen, touch of pollen,
words of pollen, perfume of pollen,
world of golden pollen,
and she breathes and is the golden pollen,
all around, golden,
and says
it has only just begun.

With the Lion

It's three, moonlight on the sheet,
I'm reaching out for you
across the bed, my voice
suddenly asking for you,
as if saying
it out loud and reaching
out could make it be.

Breathe and take
the loss, it was
always going to come
and here it is,
knowing now what I had.

Breathe with the lion.
Somewhere there is
a lion, breathing in
the night.
A lion in the night. Breathe
with the lion.

Breathe with
the mother under
the stars
and the plastic and cardboard,
praying for her children
for what won't be. Lost.

Breathe with the child
who doesn't know,
will never know,
will never be full,
or even empty,
her eyes are my eyes,
Breathe with the child
who will never know.
Never.

Breathe for those
who can't remember,
who move a little more quickly
than the rest of us
to the moment only,
breathe with them
moment to moment
as they breathe, forgotten
even to themselves. Breathe.
With the forgotten.

With the forgotten.
It won't be long.
Breathe out the expanse
of your heart.

With the lion
in the dark.

Breathe away
through to the world.
The world is breathing you.
You are the world,
the world is you,
this loss, this expanse
beyond loss, this,
that has been
with you your whole life.
Breathe with lion.

Glad

I am tired.
How could it
be otherwise?
What I thought
I understood
has faded
like fog.
I see
what I have
not seen before.

Rejoice and
be glad.
That is
what comes
to mind
in these
new
early mornings

when I am
returned to
original
solitude.

I do not want
to be without
her,
but,
I am
without her.
I see now
what we were.
It wasn't
everything,
but it was,
nearly.
Opened to
the immensity
of the loss,
I see
the immensity
of what was.

Rejoice
and be
glad.
She was the doe
of the psalms,
Solomon's song,
my song.

Immaculate. Increasing.

We became
the shining, deep-
rooted
tree.
The life-shimmering
tree.
The powerful tree.
The indomitable
tree,
the undulating
root deep sunken
flowering, fruit-bearing
tree
of my dream,

the dream
of our
shared
intertwined will.

Everything has its
time.
Every tree has its
time,
Passages begin
and end,
and begin and end
again.

Defiled. Decreasing.

As I went
to bring in
the empty
garbage can
from the street
this morning,
one of her
discarded shoes
had fallen
into the dirt
beside the can,
it was pink.

I could have fallen
to the ground
there, but
I didn't.
Though I
have
fallen to
the ground
before and
I will fall
there
again.
The low-slung
Time-dried
pink shoe
for her
slender foot

in the dirt.

It is
the totality of
our life
together.

But this
time-dried
shoe of
our youth
in the
dirt
cannot
be
an altar.
It is not
graspable.
In her
best mind,
even afraid,
she would
want me to
go on.
She would
send me on.
I know that.

Her mind
is gone.
We are
broken,
our long
bright passage
diverges
here.

No divergence.
No convergence.

No other moments
possible,
without this
moment,
no hello,
no goodbye.
Never being together,
always being together.

We two,
we became
the shimmering tree.

Rejoice,

my beloved,

and

in your
heart of hearts,
in the heart
of hearts

be

forever glad.

The Light Years

Years ago, when we descended the slope toward the cavernous entrance to Yad Vashem, the Holocaust memorial in Jerusalem, I looked up and saw on the stone archway above me a bas relief of two young brothers who had been murdered. They looked to be about the same age as our sons, whom we had left at home.

I felt a great, explosive expansion in my chest, and I collapsed to my knees, weeping. It was completely unanticipated, one of the two times I have cried as an adult. The other time was for joy. My wife reached down to help me back up, but it took a minute.

We don't take the soft fall light here in the desert for granted. The desert can be hard, and the unbridled, unfiltered light of the hot season persists for months and is as much a marker of the environment as the heat itself. Toward the fall, it can still reach midsummer-like temperatures, but even so, the slanted light brings its own relief, its own anticipation.

I was at a local café recently in the late afternoon, seated on the patio beneath the shade of the citrus trees, enjoying that very light. It was just me and a couple with three young children at the other end of the patio. Two of the children were sisters, maybe five and three. Their little brother was in a stroller at his mother's feet. His mother was dressed conservatively and wearing a hijab.

The father is a man I had seen before several times at another café. Sometimes, he was there with a man who appeared to be his brother and a small, dignified older man whom they seemed to be caring for. Their father, I supposed. They spoke Arabic to one another.

Perhaps the sisters were inspired by the light, as I was, but that is not to say they needed it as much as I did. They were joyous, running up the two steps leading into the cafe and then jumping off them in perfect unison, again and again. Then, suddenly, they would stop and chase the pigeons, who would then chase them back, and the girls would scream and run away themselves. Then, they pursed their lips and made a little summoning sound, a gesture they had clearly seen demonstrated by someone else, probably their mother or father. When it didn't work, they turned their ecstatic attention back to the steps.

The mother and father weren't talking, and they weren't on their phones. They were watching their children in the soft relief of this new light. Being with their children in the soft relief of this new light in the shade of the citrus trees on this fall afternoon in the desert.

Suddenly, I felt an explosive expansion in my chest and felt tears forming when I realized that hundreds of children just like those little girls were dying in Gaza every day, even as we sat in the light. The father would occasionally make eye contact, and I sensed we both had the same understanding. All children just want to jump up and down the steps and chase the pigeons. It was October 10, 2023.

The dead don't have a stake anymore. They know that grief looks the same on every face. They know that all atrocities are born of the same mother and father. They know that one barbarism follows another, that hatred feeds on hatred, and that this terrified, grasping, retaliatory brutality is our undoing.

If you don't think so, ask them. If you listen carefully, quiet yourself, they will tell you that truth and others from over the light years of their appearances and disappearances.

There was a Zen master who had suffered a lot and given a lot, more than most. At the end, he said, "The only thing worthy of you is compassion—invincible, limitless, unconditional. Hatred will never let you face the beast in man."

Just because it is unattainable for almost all of us, myself included, doesn't make it any less true.

No Words

Oh, these days,
these days are
neither long nor short.
I have taken to lying
on the wooden floor,
the ninety-year-old
wooden floor.
My bones need
settling, and they
descend down
toward its no-nonsense
realignment and
its open-hearted reception.
There are no words
that can capture
an actual life.

There aren't enough
of them, there isn't
enough time, there isn't
the adequacy,
so, to look up from this floor
and to see the spider,
apex of a
million generations,
making its way
across the ceiling,
inch by inch,
across the crevices
and rises in the stucco,
to know that it is
my brother, carefully
crossing the hard territory,
is more than to say
it is my brother.
To know is the language
of dreaming.
If you are unsure
what somebody means,
means to you, conjure
or wait on a dream of their
falling, beyond your
grasp, and the
wordless language
of knowing will startle you
envelop you, inform you,

and you will understand
something of your
shrouded life making
its way through the
crevices and rises
in this hard territory.
Oh, here is change
at the door.
We know when
it arrives, no need
for an announcement, no
need for a ceremony,
it had been here,
we know, but
pretend not to,
for some time.
The bristle cone pines
high up
in the western mountains
are the oldest living things,
on Earth, some nearly
five thousand years old.
They have made
every adjustment,
every adaptation,

high up there
in the clear and seldom-
disturbed air, expanded,
contracted, allowed parts
of themselves to die,
chosen not to be grand.
Nothing gets that far
without what I suppose
must be called
humility, gratitude
for the opportunity.
There are no words
for them or for us. Somewhere
deep in their millennial
heartwood they choose.
Conditions, fire, drought,
disease, other creatures,
earthquakes, landslides,
loss of an ancient companion,
all manner of catastrophes
have challenged them,
been the change presenting,
questioning their being.
And they have chosen
again, again and again,
in their wordless way,
to love.

Lotus River

I heard a man
speaking on the radio,
humility unadorned.
He worked with tortured monks and nuns
who could no longer meditate,
their quieted breath summoning memories,
thoughts they could no longer bear
or control.

He advised them, he said,
to transform memories, as they arose, into
lotus blossoms,
and to place them on a river.
The river.

Think about it.
Lowering yourself down onto
the sandy bank of the pure-faced,
black river,
placing lotus blossoms,
one after another,
onto the silent, moving sheen.

If it were the only thing
you ever did
in your life,
it would be
enough.

American Beast

It was conceived in banality,
comforted with lullabies of brutality
it is the slouching rough beast,
it doesn't care what you think.

It speaks the language of inanity,
feeds and grows giant on our insanity.
It chews and marauds, cares not the least
what you do or if it's poison you drink.

The beast can't see, totally blind,
it neither sees nor feels any other kind,
in its mindless rage of consumption
it mangles and rips sad gratitude.

Teeth bared, screeching, certain and confined
within the flickering walls of a clenched mind,
it sows fear and waters destruction,
has never heard and never will the beatitudes.

Empty, empty at its foul and solitary core,
everyone it touches becomes a whore.
High on triumph, bedazzled by glitter,
they pay homage to the sparkling lie.

The beast cannot reveal what is in store,
morphs the world to its will and then to war,
it grows strong as all others cower and wither,
preens, gloats as the future and our children die.

Save yourself and everyone else, say amen,
there'll be no salvation from Bethlehem.
No time for television, doubt, or hesitation,
enter the raging gyre, fight your way through.

Take the knife you've had since God knows when,
slash that beast with knife and righteous omen,
feel the blade enter your chest, it is our creation,
the beast is us, reckoned sad and brutal true.

Man in the Neighborhood

Let me tell you something. I can't tell you in its totality. Nothing can be told in its totality.

There is a woman in our neighborhood, an old woman, eight-nine. She is wizened. I mean worn, worn is better, worn like fine sand grooved and rippled by rain or worn smooth and rough in the right places by the elements, like a thousand-year-old tree. In her case, a tree that interacted with conditions and stayed small, maybe five feet, maybe ninety, ninety-five pounds.

She has had a knee replacement, but if you see her walking from a distance, she could be thirty. Her sexuality seems intact, you can feel it from her, not in a salacious way, just that it is there, never departed, perhaps not even diminished. Her deeply lined face is an artifact of vitality, humor, determination. She was a nurse.

Bruni laughs and blushes like a girl still, hand coming up to her face, her gap-toothed smile still bright, still hers, Mexican, Indian, American, all the strengths collected in her. A doña, a funny one, an open one, no special airs or lace mantillas for her. Her hands are adapted, roots smoothed over and perfectly formed by exposure.

She is alone now. Rudy is gone, the tall, graceful man, a vaquero, a natural aristocrat, one of the good aristocrats of the land. Rudy, with the fine features of bemused kindness and patience, who came back from the war in Korea, saw her at the hospital, and then went back to the war, survived, wrote her, came back again. They were married for sixty-four years. Four children, grandchildren. They loved to dance together. And they walked.

Sometimes, before Rudy started to decline, I would see them out before the sun came up, walking eight or ten miles together, hand in hand. Then again at night. He had been a fireman, retired, and went to the university to study art. He drew, painted, and painted, not interested in judging, it seemed, but in seeing. Even when he began to fade, the quietness of his acceptance, the reflected light of that in his eyes, became more luminous. Who knows what he was in his totality? What any of us are in our totality?

We saw Bruni walking in the rain at twilight a few days ago, coming toward us with her confounding energy that, from a distance, could be a thirty-year-old's. She embraced us, laughed a little, and said she had to get out of the house and away from all the tales of suffering from family, coming in over the phone.

"I'm ready to go now," she said.

"Are you?" I asked.

"Yes, I'm ready," but nothing more than that.

It began to rain a little harder, and she pulled up the hood of her sweatshirt. "I better get in," she said, and we all embraced there again in the rain.

She didn't mention what she had told me a month earlier. I was just inside her front door at the time. Her home is simple, clean, Rudy's art on the walls.

She took my arm at the elbow. "I want to tell you something," she said. She seemed shaken, a little emptied. "You know Rudy died here," she continued. "We kept him here at home, my son and I, for three days. Rudy had a professor, and we used to take care of his two daughters. They were like grandchildren to us. Rudy wasn't talking, but he kept saying the name of the older daughter. They had been really close. So finally, I called her dad, and he told her, and she came over to see him. She put her head on his shoulder, and he put his hand on her head, and she cried and cried."

Bruni was still holding on to my arm. "On the last day, I was sitting beside the bed, and I looked over, and Rudy was floating just above the bed. I looked over at my son. He was standing, and he looked at me, and we didn't know what to do. Even Rudy looked surprised," she said. "He did it two more times, and then he died. I don't know what to think. He was a very fine man, a very good man."

Rudy, floating just over the bed, surprised, dying, befuddled. I don't know what to think, either.

I don't know what our totality embraces. There are days when it seems we are an accident of flesh, raw reactions, and nerves, and then there are others when I suspect it might be more than we can grasp. Now, I can feel Bruni and her rooted hand at my elbow, with deep need to tell me what she saw.

Everything

We are woven through time
together.
Now, she is in front of me
but not here.
She gave me my bright life,
but she doesn't know my name.

I always suspected
that there was no final
refuge in beauty,
but of course, we are
all hungry for it,
hoping for a ticket
to transcendence,

but it is just not the way,
is it? We marvel at
the sunset, at the
purple glisten, the interior of the plum,
at the Cosmic Cliffs
in the Carina Nebula,
which look like the Catalina mountains
she has always loved and
still recognizes,
at the unspeakably good
fortune of having a
wonderful life,
but then, while
raking the mesquite pods
in a state of psychic exhaustion,
I see that the desiccated
lizard at the foot
of the pond
is no longer iridescent,
and that is a fact.
Is everything in everything?

The cosmic cliffs
in the Catalinas,
the death gray in the iridescent,
the Carina Nebula always present
in our tired, shadowed mind,
the beauty that stirs our hope,
the hope itself there in despair?

Marcus Aurelius was mostly right,
the goodbye was always in the hello,
the loss always was in the gain,
the wrong appetites cannot be satisfied,
bow your head to that only,
do what must be done,
receive and relinquish
with the sad grace
of an enlightened but impoverished king.

Diamond

Opening, not closing,
going out,
but not away.

Long gone down,
on the inside,
not the outside.

Throwing out,
paring to the blood
of iron marrow.

Seeing what is gone
is not the same
as hanging on.

Seeing what is,
must be done.
Done is done.

The sunlit glass
of my life in the
hand of Christ.

Life is effort,
breathe, breathing,
light, striving.

In the womb,
I had a diamond
in my mind,

there, in the
moon-washed sea
of everything,
without a name,
without a memory,
I was brilliant.

Reaching

Sometimes, the dying reach out
to a person only they can see.
Sometimes the living do, too.
Late, after midnight,
reaching across the bed
for what is not there,
for what cannot be recovered,
the reaching can retrieve it
put it in mind and body
again, for just the briefest of moments,
but
not to have.
Reaching.
That's what the dying are doing.
The living, too.

The stars are not indifferent.
Blind, brilliant, and beguiling
as they are, the lords above,
across all time,
unchanging to us until they die,

collapsing into themselves
or flashing out into quantum,
turning dark, disintegrating,
beautiful and beguiling as they are,
they are just residue,

the residue
of a being
that proclaims itself
alive to the universe,

that can understand
its place like a leaf
on a tree,
fluorescing, evanescing,
that completes the cycle,
that can reach for another
who is not there,
after midnight,
that longs, gives thanks,

and

can love.

Can love.

Can love.

The Bright Language

In the tangle of tomato leaves and blossoms,
standing in the early-morning spring sun,
I find the fear is now gone, a weave
of my own making, and the air is cool.

The soil speaks its own bright language,
the language of these and those, things
that were formally encased, now not,
alternately sterile, then fertile.

Repository of bodies, suns, and the ages,
the world-traveled soil, present at the start,
its presence beyond all grasping.
This longing, what discipline it needs.

Practice for death, take dirt into your hand,
raise it to your chest at the heart,
give thanks, bless the Earth in entirety,
and see those who forgive in all directions.

Those stepped out from body and meme,
released from knowing and unknowing,
those who inhabit memory and soil,
water, sun, mind, and the air around.

The bright language sounds a hum
of energy and release, a bee moves
in the green tangle toward a flower,
with intention, and the air is cool.

Meditation

Wouldn't we be better off
if we faced the one certain truth
that we have no idea
who we are, what we are,
where we are, except for right here,
that we and all beings
inhabit that truth
despite what we who speak
and think might say and believe,
and that, once we get over
our trembling,
might it not be best
to acknowledge that,
except for each other,
we are alone,
inseparable and responsible?

Interesting thought, but,
what would it mean
to the grandfather
in Acapulco who identified
his seventeen- and eighteen-year-old grandsons'
bodies after they had been
mistaken for the wrong
brothers and garroted
to death with wire?
What, for that matter,
would it mean
to the men who did it?

What would it mean
to the mother in Tucson
who came home from
the theater to find
her fifteen-year-old son
hanging dead from
a tree in the backyard?

Or to the Syrian father
watching his children drown?

To the nation,
whose twelve-year-olds,
playing alone in the park,
are shot by the police,
blood bright on the snow?

To the mute young woman
in the Congo, raped, tied
to a tree, forced to watch
her toddler
being disemboweled?
And to those
hungry ghosts who
did that, from whom,
in body, place, and history,
we are inseparable,
what would
the one certain truth
mean to them?

What name is it
that we call out to
in the night
when the
one certain truth
fails us?

Is it father
that we call for?
Mother?
Dear Holy Father?
Dear Holy Mother?
Should we whisper
there in the dark
or with a candle lit,
by ourselves, in ourselves,
for our ancestors
to come quickly
to our side?

Should we there,
in the dark
or in the candlelight,

consent to the body's
insistence, its calamities,
feel ourselves in time,
the past, present
and future of our
life, whole, all in one,
an integrity,
and from there, ready,
wait like a mountain
for the sound
of the true name?

Beachcomber

For Tunisian fisherman,
Chammesdine Marzoug

The sound of his steps
through the sand
travels beyond speed
to all of the galaxies,
the Tunisian fisherman
combing the beach
for profundities
that have tumbled in,
as nude as seaweed,
meticulously undressed
by the breathing tides.

Profundities that had
favorite shirts,
faces of wonder,
appetites, a taste for rice
and mango, for
enough to eat, for
a home, for a job,
for knowing,
for the sound of a bird,
for life,
for being seen,
for a book,
for a song, for a dance,
for mother, father,
brother, sister, lover,
wife, husband,
son and daughter.

He washes them,
puts them in a body bag
and takes them
to town so that
their destinies,
as flotsam,
can be recorded,

brings them back to
the seaside cemetery
on ground he claimed
beside the landfill,
sees them, buries them,
marks, marks
their graves with
painted rocks,
cement fragments,
a fresh flower,
small toys
for the children,
400, twelve more last week,

the sound of his spade
splitting the sand
traveling to all
of the galaxies,

beyond speed.

Burying the Cat

"Immaculate or defiled,
Increasing or decreasing,
these are just concepts in our mind.
The reality of interbeing is unsurpassed."
—Thich Nhat Hanh
"Using the Toilet," *Gathas for Daily Living*

A killer, sunworshipper, a cat unperturbed
by any possibility other than perfect cathood,
sleek prince of the yards, acrobat, assassin,
even of the ruby-throated hummingbird
suspended just this much too long
at the dangling, blood trumpet of penstemon.
When I carried your impossibly light
limpness to your grave, a lizard
bolted past, still terrified. Rightly so.

Wasted to the bone. Half your jaw gone,
drool of blood-stained mucus trailing
your unsteadiness, forepaws encrusted
with the uncleanable, your fur dulled
and laid like oily cloth over jumble of bolts,
sharp-ended screws, jagged scrap.

But that is not all that we buried.

It is not just a cat that is put down, after all. A cat
    was born in our youngest son's bed, eighteen
    years ago on a flowered sheet.
Unexpected, like a miracle then.
We wrapped him for burial in a remnant, flowers
    holding their color pretty well.
A cat died. No big deal.
The world should stop, take notice, however.

Each shovelful of earth falls like a telegram stop.
All will vanish. Stop.
Loss will be total and complete. Stop. No tear, no
    laugh. Stop.
No death, no birth. Stop.
One thing becomes another. Stop. Love best you
    can. Stop.
Love best you can. Stop. Love best you can. Stop.

Stop.

I found nothing.
Nothing, in fact, found me.
Everything is here.

This haiku is both epigraph and epilogue. I revisited all of the pieces between them as I prepared this book. Some of them were written in the last couple of years, and some from within the last ten or so years. In one case, one poem was written over fifty years ago. I recognize myself in these poems and prose pieces across all those years, trying to make sense of it all, trying to come to terms with the profundity of being alive, the profundity of gain and loss that belongs to us all.

I am glad you are here. I hope, between epigraph and epilogue, you see something of yourself, something that gives you strength. And that you see me, as well, as someone here in the world and the wonder, in the bewilderment and the horror, alongside you.

—G.H.

About the Author

Greg Hart lives in Tucson, Arizona. He has two sons, Abraham John and Nathaniel Joseph; three daughters by choice and good fortune, Alexa, Megan and Rosario; three grandchildren, Tallulah, Eli, and Alex; two brothers, Matthew and Douglas; a sister and a brother by another mother, Susan and Gerald; a mother and brother by marriage, Jo Margaret and Craig; and many other beloved friends and family.

www.ingramcontent.com/pod-product-compliance
Lightning Source LLC
Chambersburg PA
CBHW031336060726
47590CB00007B/2493